B

ALL THE WORLD

ALL THE
WORLD OVER

NOTES FROM ALASKA

John Muir

SIERRA CLUB BOOKS ⟨⟩ SAN FRANCISCO

A Sierra Club Pathstone Edition™

The Sierra Club, founded in 1892 by John Muir, has devoted itself to the study and protection of the earth's scenic and ecological resources—mountains, wetlands, woodlands, wild shores and rivers, deserts and plains. The publishing program of the Sierra Club offers books to the public as a non-profit educational service in the hope that they may enlarge the public's understanding of the Club's basic concerns. The point of view expressed in each book, however, does not necessarily represent that of the Club. The Sierra Club has some sixty chapters coast to coast, in Canada, Hawaii, and Alaska. For information about how you may participate in its programs to preserve wilderness and the quality of life, please address inquiries to Sierra Club, 730 Polk Street, San Francisco, CA 94109.

Library of Congress Cataloging-in-Publication Data

Muir, John, 1838–1914.

[Travels in Alaska]

All the world over : notes from Alaska / John Muir.

p.   cm.

Originally published: Travels in Alaska. Boston :
Houghton Mifflin, 1915.

ISBN 0-87156-853-5 (pbk. : alk. paper)

1. Muir, John, 1838–1914—Journeys—Alaska.
2. Alaska—Description and travel—1867–1896.
3. Naturalists—United States—Biography.   I. Title.

QH31.M9A3   1996
508.798'092—dc20

[B]   95-25688

Production by Susan Ristow · Cover and book design by Amy Evans
Composition by Wilsted & Taylor

Printed in the United States on acid-free paper containing a minimum of 50% recovered waste paper, of which at least 10% of the fiber content is post-consumer waste

10   9   8   7   6   5   4   3   2   1

CONTENTS

One bird, a thrush, embroidered the silence with cheery notes, making the solitude familiar and sweet, while the solemn monotone of the stream sifting through the woods seemed like the very voice of God, humanized, terrestrialized, and entering one's heart as to a home prepared for it. Go where we will, all the world over, we seem to have been there before.

JOHN MUIR

ALEXANDER
ARCHIPELAGO

To the lover of pure wildness Alaska is one of the most wonderful countries in the world. No excursion that I know of may be made into any other American wilderness where so marvelous an abundance of noble, newborn scenery is so charmingly brought to view as on the trip through the Alexander Archipelago to Fort Wrangell and Sitka. Gazing from the deck of the steamer, one is borne smoothly over calm blue waters, through the midst of countless forest-clad islands. The ordinary discomforts of a sea voyage are not felt, for nearly all the whole long way is on inland waters that are about as waveless as rivers and lakes. So numerous are the islands that they seem to have been sown broadcast; long tapering vistas between the largest of them open in every direction.

Day after day in the fine weather we enjoyed, we seemed to float in true fairyland, each succeeding view seeming more and more beautiful, the one we chanced to have before us the most surprisingly beautiful of all. Never before this had I been embosomed in scenery so hopelessly beyond description. To sketch picturesque bits, definitely bounded, is comparatively easy—a lake in the woods, a glacier meadow, or a cascade in its dell; or even a grand masterview of mountains beheld from some commanding outlook after climbing from height to height above the forests. These may be attempted, and more or less telling pictures made of them; but in these coast landscapes there is such indefinite, on-leading expansiveness, such a multitude of features without apparent redundance, their lines graduating delicately into one another in endless succession, while the whole is so fine, so tender, so ethereal, that all penwork seems hopelessly unavailing. Tracing shining ways through fiord and sound, past forests and waterfalls, islands and mountains and far azure headlands, it seems as if surely we must at length reach the very paradise of the poets, the abode of the blessed.

Some idea of the wealth of this scenery may be gained from the fact that the coast-line of Alaska is about twenty-six thousand miles long, more than twice as long as all the rest of the United States. The islands of the Alexander Archipelago, with the straits, channels, canals, sounds, passages, and fiords, form an intricate web of land and water embroidery sixty or seventy miles wide, fringing the lofty icy chain of coast mountains from Puget Sound to Cook Inlet; and, with infinite variety, the general pattern is harmonious throughout its whole extent of nearly a thousand miles. Here you glide into a narrow channel hemmed in by mountain walls, forested down to the water's edge, where there is no distant view, and your attention is concentrated on the objects close about you—the crowded spires of the spruces and hemlocks rising higher and higher on the steep green slopes; stripes of paler green where winter avalanches have cleared away the trees, allowing grasses and willows to spring up; zigzags of cascades appearing and disappearing among the bushes and trees; short, steep glens with brawling streams hidden beneath alder and dogwood, seen only where they emerge on the brown algæ of the shore; and retreating hollows, with lingering snow-banks marking the fountains of ancient glaciers. The steamer is often so near the shore that you may distinctly see the cones clustered on the tops of the trees, and the ferns and bushes at their feet.

But new scenes are brought to view with magical rapidity. Rounding some bossy cape, the eye is called away into far-reaching vistas, bounded on either hand by headlands in charming array, one dipping gracefully beyond another and growing fainter and more ethereal in the distance. The tranquil channel stretching river-like between, may be stirred here and there by the silvery plashing of upspringing salmon, or by flocks of white gulls floating like waterlilies among the sun spangles; while mellow, tempered sunshine is streaming over all, blending sky, land, and water in pale, misty blue. Then, while you are dreamily gazing into the depths of this leafy ocean lane, the little steamer, seeming hardly larger than a duck, turning into some passage not visible until the moment of entering it, glides into a wide expanse—a sound filled with islands, sprinkled and clustered in forms and compositions such as nature alone can invent; some of them so small the trees growing on them seem like single handfuls culled from the neighboring woods and set in the water to keep them fresh, while here and there at wide intervals you may notice bare rocks just above the water, mere dots punctuating grand, outswelling sentences of islands.

The variety we find, both as to the contours and the collocation of the islands, is due chiefly to differences in the structure and composition of their rocks, and the unequal glacial denudation different portions of the coast were subjected to. This influence must have been especially heavy toward the end of the glacial period, when the main ice-sheet began to break up into separate glaciers. Moreover, the mountains of the larger islands nourished local glaciers, some of them of considerable size, which sculptured their summits and sides, forming in some cases wide cirques with cañons or valleys leading down from them into the channels and sounds. These causes have produced much of the bewildering variety of which nature is so fond, but none the less will the studious observer see the underlying harmony— the general trend of the islands in the direction of the flow of the main ice-mantle from the mountains of the Coast Range, more or less varied by subordinate foothill ridges and mountains. Furthermore, all the islands, great and small, as well as the headlands and promontories of the mainland, are seen to have a rounded, over-rubbed appearance produced by the over-sweeping ice-flood during the period of greatest glacial abundance.

The canals, channels, straits, passages, sounds, etc., are subordinate to the same glacial conditions in their forms, trends, and extent as those which determined the forms, trends, and distribution of the land-masses, their basins being the parts of the pre-glacial margin of the continent, eroded to varying depths below sea-level, and into which, of course, the ocean waters flowed as the ice was melted out of them. Had the general glacial denudation been much less, these ocean ways over which we are sailing would have been valleys and cañons and lakes; and the islands rounded hills and ridges, landscapes with undulating features like those found above sea-level wherever the rocks and glacial conditions are similar. In general, the island-bound channels are like rivers, not only in separate reaches as seen from the deck of a vessel, but continuously so for hundreds of miles in the case of the longest of them. The tide-currents, the fresh driftwood, the inflowing streams, and the luxuriant foliage of the out-leaning trees on the shores make this resemblance all the more complete. The largest islands look like part of the mainland in any view to be had of them from the ship, but far the greater number are small, and appreciable as islands, scores of them being less than a mile long. These the eye easily takes in and revels in their beauty with ever fresh delight. In their relations to each other the indi-vidual members of a group have evidently been de-rived from the same general rock-mass, yet they never seem broken or abridged in any way as to their contour lines, however abruptly they may dip their sides. Viewed one by one, they seem detached beauties, like extracts from a poem, while, from the completeness of their lines and the way that their trees are arranged, each seems a finished stanza in itself. Contemplating the arrangement of the trees on these small islands, a distinct impression is produced of their having been sorted and harmonized as to size like a well-balanced bouquet. On some of the smaller tufted islets a group of tapering spruces is planted in the middle, and two smaller groups that evidently correspond with each other are planted on the ends at about equal distances from the central group; or the whole appears as one group with marked fringing trees that match each other spreading around the sides, like flowers leaning outward against the rim of a vase. These harmonious tree relations are so constant that they evidently are the result of design, as much so as the arrangement of the feathers of birds or the scales of fishes.

Thus perfectly beautiful are these blessed evergreen islands, and their beauty is the beauty of youth, for though the freshness of their verdure must be ascribed to the bland moisture with which they are bathed from warm ocean-currents, the very exis-

tence of the islands, their features, finish, and peculiar distribution, are all immediately referable to
ice-action during the great glacial winter just now
drawing to a close.

✳

We arrived at Wrangell July 14, and after a short stop
of a few hours went on to Sitka and returned on the
20th to Wrangell, the most inhospitable place at first
sight I had ever seen. The little steamer that had been
my home in the wonderful trip through the archipelago, after taking the mail, departed on her return to
Portland, and as I watched her gliding out of sight in
the dismal blurring rain, I felt strangely lonesome.
The friend that had accompanied me thus far now left
for his home in San Francisco, with two other interesting travelers who had made the trip for health and
scenery, while my fellow passengers, the missionaries, went direct to the Presbyterian home in the old
fort. There was nothing like a tavern or lodging-
house in the village, nor could I find any place in the
stumpy, rocky, boggy ground about it that looked dry
enough to camp on until I could find a way into the
wilderness to begin my studies. Every place within
a mile or two of the town seemed strangely shelter-
less and inhospitable, for all the trees had long ago

been felled for building-timber and firewood. At the worst, I thought, I could build a bark hut on a hill back of the village, where something like a forest loomed dimly through the draggled clouds.

I had already seen some of the high glacier-bearing mountains in distant views from the steamer, and was anxious to reach them. A few whites of the village, with whom I entered into conversation, warned me that the Indians were a bad lot, not to be trusted, that the woods were well-nigh impenetrable, and that I could go nowhere without a canoe. On the other hand, these natural difficulties made the grand wild country all the more attractive, and I determined to get into the heart of it somehow or other with a bag of hardtack, trusting to my usual good luck. My present difficulty was in finding a first base camp. My only hope was on the hill. When I was strolling past the old fort I happened to meet one of the missionaries, who kindly asked me where I was going to take up my quarters.

"I don't know," I replied. "I have not been able to find quarters of any sort. The top of that little hill over there seems the only possible place."

He then explained that every room in the mission house was full, but he thought I might obtain leave to spread my blanket in a carpenter-shop belonging to the mission. Thanking him, I ran down to the sloppy wharf for my little bundle of baggage, laid it on the shop floor, and felt glad and snug among the dry, sweet-smelling shavings.

The carpenter was at work on a new Presbyterian mission building, and when he came in I explained that Dr. Jackson had suggested that I might be allowed to sleep on the floor, and after I assured him that I would not touch his tools or be in his way, he goodnaturedly gave me the freedom of the shop and also of his small private side room where I would find a wash-basin.

I was here only one night, however, for Mr. Vanderbilt, a merchant, who with his family occupied the best house in the fort, hearing that one of the late arrivals, whose business none seemed to know, was compelled to sleep in the carpenter-shop, paid me a good-Samaritan visit and after a few explanatory words on my glacier and forest studies, with fine hospitality offered me a room and a place at his table. Here I found a real home, with freedom to go on all sorts of excursions as opportunity offered. Annie Vanderbilt, a little doctor of divinity two years old, ruled the household with love sermons and kept it warm.

Mr. Vanderbilt introduced me to prospectors and

traders and some of the most influential of the Indians. I visited the mission school and the home for Indian girls kept by Mrs. MacFarland, and made short excursions to the nearby forests and streams, and studied the rate of growth of the different species of trees and their age, counting the annual rings on stumps in the large clearings made by the military when the fort was occupied, causing wondering speculation among the Wrangell folk, as was reported by Mr. Vanderbilt.

"What can the fellow be up to?" they inquired. "He seems to spend most of his time among stumps and weeds. I saw him the other day on his knees, looking at a stump as if he expected to find gold in it. He seems to have no serious object whatever."

One night when a heavy rainstorm was blowing I unwittingly caused a lot of wondering excitement among the whites as well as the superstitious Indians. Being anxious to see how the Alaska trees behave in storms and hear the songs they sing, I stole quietly away through the gray drenching blast to the hill back of the town, without being observed. Night was falling when I set out and it was pitch dark when I reached the top. The glad, rejoicing storm in glorious voice was singing through the woods, noble compensation for mere body discomfort. But I wanted a fire, a big one, to see as well as hear how the storm and trees were behaving. After long, patient groping I found a little dry punk in a hollow trunk and carefully stored it beside my matchbox and an inch or two of candle in an inside pocket that the rain had not yet reached; then, wiping some dead twigs and whittling them into thin shavings, stored them with the punk. I then made a little conical bark hut about a foot high, and, carefully leaning over it and sheltering it as much as possible from the driving rain, I wiped and stored a lot of dead twigs, lighted the candle, and set it in the hut, carefully added pinches of punk and shavings, and at length got a little blaze, by the light of which I gradually added larger shavings, then twigs all set on end astride the inner flame, making the little hut higher and wider. Soon I had light enough to enable me to select the best dead branches and large sections of bark, which were set on end, gradually increasing the height and corresponding light of the hut fire. A considerable area was thus well lighted, from which I gathered abundance of wood, and kept adding to the fire until it had a strong, hot heart and sent up a pillar of flame thirty or forty feet high, illuminating a wide circle in spite of the rain, and casting a red glare into the flying clouds. Of all the thousands of camp-fires I have elsewhere built none was just like this one, rejoicing in triumphant strength and beauty in the heart of the rain-laden gale. It was wonderful,—the illumined rain and clouds mingled together and the trees glowing against the jet background, the colors of the mossy, lichened trunks with sparkling streams pouring down the furrows of the bark, and the gray-bearded old patriarchs bowing low and chanting in passionate worship!

My fire was in all its glory about midnight, and, having made a bark shed to shelter me from the rain and partially dry my clothing, I had nothing to do but look and listen and join the trees in their hymns and prayers.

Neither the great white heart of the fire nor the quivering enthusiastic flames shooting aloft like auroral lances could be seen from the village on account of the trees in front of it and its being back a little way over the brow of the hill; but the light in the clouds made a great show, a portentous sign in the stormy heavens unlike anything ever before seen or heard of in Wrangell. Some wakeful Indians, happening to see it about midnight, in great alarm aroused the Collector of Customs and begged him to go to the missionaries and get them to pray away the frightful omen, and inquired anxiously whether white men had ever seen anything like that sky-fire, which instead of being quenched by the rain was burning brighter and brighter. The Collector said he had heard of such strange fires, and this one he thought might perhaps be what the white man called a "volcano, or an *ignis fatuus.*" When Mr. Young was called from his bed to pray, he, too, confoundedly astonished and at a loss for any sort of explanation, confessed that he had never seen anything like it in the sky or anywhere else in such cold wet weather, but that it was probably some sort of spontaneous combustion "that the white man called St. Elmo's fire, or Will-of-the-wisp." These explanations, though not convincingly clear, perhaps served to veil their own astonishment and in some measure to diminish the superstitious fears of the natives; but from what I heard, the few whites who happened to see the strange light wondered about as wildly as the Indians.

I have enjoyed thousands of camp-fires in all sorts of weather and places, warm-hearted, short-flamed, friendly little beauties glowing in the dark on open spots in high Sierra gardens, daisies and lilies circled about them, gazing like enchanted children; and large fires in silver fir forests, with spires of flame towering like the trees about them, and sending up multitudes of starry sparks to enrich the sky; and still greater fires on the mountains in winter, changing camp climate to summer, and making the frosty snow look like beds of white flowers, and oftentimes mingling their swarms of swift-flying sparks with falling snow-crystals when the clouds were in bloom. But this Wrangell camp-fire, my first in Alaska, I shall always remember for its triumphant storm-defying grandeur, and the wondrous beauty of the psalm-singing, lichen-painted trees which it brought to light.

WRANGELL ISLAND

W<small>RANGELL ISLAND</small> IS about fourteen miles long, separated from the mainland by a narrow channel or fiord, and trending in the direction of the flow of the ancient ice-sheet. Like all its neighbors, it is densely forested down to the water's edge with trees that never seem to have suffered from thirst or fire or the axe of the lumberman in all their long century lives. Beneath soft, shady clouds, with abundance of rain, they flourish in wonderful strength and beauty to a good old age, while the many warm days, half cloudy, half clear, and the little groups of pure sun-days enable them to ripen their cones and send myriads of seeds flying every autumn to insure the permanence of the forests and feed the multitude of animals.

The Wrangell village was a rough place. No mining hamlet in the placer gulches of California, nor any backwoods village I ever saw, approached it in picturesque, devil-may-care *abandon*. It was a lawless draggle of wooden huts and houses, built in crooked lines, wrangling around the boggy shore of the island for a mile or so in the general form of the letter S, without the slightest subordination to the points of the compass or to building laws of any kind. Stumps and logs, like precious monuments, adorned its two streets, each stump and log, on account of the moist climate, moss-grown and tufted with grass and bushes, but muddy on the sides below the limit of the bogline. The ground in general was an oozy, mossy bog on a foundation of jagged rocks, full of concealed pitholes. These picturesque rock, bog, and stump obstructions, however, were not so very much in the way, for there were no wagons or carriages there. There was not a horse on the island. The domestic animals were represented by chickens, a lonely cow, a few sheep, and hogs of a breed well calculated to deepen and complicate the mud of the streets.

Most of the permanent residents of Wrangell were engaged in trade. Some little trade was carried on in fish and furs, but most of the quickening business of the place was derived from the Cassiar gold-mines, some two hundred and fifty or three hundred miles inland, by way of the Stickeen River and Dease

Lake. Two stern-wheel steamers plied on the river between Wrangell and Telegraph Creek at the head of navigation, a hundred and fifty miles from Wrangell, carrying freight and passengers and connecting with pack-trains for the mines. These placer mines, on tributaries of the Mackenzie River, were discovered in the year 1874. About eighteen hundred miners and prospectors were said to have passed through Wrangell that season of 1879, about half of them being Chinamen. Nearly a third of this whole number set out from here in the month of February, traveling on the Stickeen River, which usually remains safely frozen until toward the end of April. The main body of the miners, however, went up on the steamers in May and June. On account of the severe winters they were all compelled to leave the mines the end of September. Perhaps about two thirds of them passed the winter in Portland and Victoria and the towns of Puget Sound. The rest remained here in Wrangell, dozing away the long winter as best they could.

Indians, mostly of the Stickeen tribe, occupied the two ends of the town, the whites, of whom there were about forty or fifty, the middle portion; but there was no determinate line of demarcation, the dwellings of the Indians being mostly as large and solidly built of logs and planks as those of the whites. Some of them were adorned with tall totem poles.

The fort was a quadrangular stockade with a dozen block and frame buildings located upon rising ground just back of the business part of the town. It was built by our Government shortly after the purchase of Alaska, and was abandoned in 1872, reoccupied by the military in 1875, and finally abandoned and sold to private parties in 1877. In the fort and about it there were a few good, clean homes, which shone all the more brightly in their sombre surroundings. The ground occupied by the fort, by being carefully leveled and drained was dry, though formerly a portion of the general swamp, showing how easily the whole town could have been improved. But in spite of disorder and squalor, shaded with clouds, washed and wiped by rain and sea winds, it was triumphantly salubrious through all the seasons. And though the houses seemed to rest uneasily among the miry rocks and stumps, squirming at all angles as if they had been tossed and twisted by earthquake shocks, and showing but little more relation to one another than may be observed among moraine boulders, Wrangell was a tranquil place. I never heard a noisy brawl in the streets, or a clap of thunder, and the waves seldom spoke much above a whisper along the beach. In summer the rain comes straight down, steamy and tepid. The clouds are usually united, filling the sky, not racing along in threatening ranks suggesting energy of an overbearing destructive kind, but forming a bland, mild, laving bath. The cloudless days are calm, pearl-gray, and brooding in tone, inclining to rest and peace; the islands seem to drowse and float on the glassy water, and in the woods scarce a leaf stirs.

The very brightest of Wrangell days are not what Californians would call bright. The tempered sunshine sifting through the moist atmosphere makes no dazzling glare, and the town, like the landscape, rests beneath a hazy, hushing, Indian-summerish spell. On the longest days the sun rises about three o'clock, but it is daybreak at midnight. The cocks crowed when they woke, without reference to the dawn, for it is never quite dark; there were only a few full-grown roosters in Wrangell, half a dozen or so, to awaken the town and give it a civilized character. After sunrise a few languid smoke-columns might be seen, telling the first stir of the people. Soon an Indian or two might be noticed here and there at the doors of their barnlike cabins, and a merchant getting ready for trade; but scarcely a sound was heard, only a dull, muffled stir gradually deepening. There were only

two white babies in the town, so far as I saw, and as
for Indian babies, they woke and ate and made no cry-
ing sound. Later you might hear the croaking of ra-
vens, and the strokes of an axe on firewood. About
eight or nine o'clock the town was awake, Indians,
mostly women and children, began to gather on the
front platforms of the half-dozen stores, sitting care-
lessly on their blankets, every other face hideously
blackened, a naked circle around the eyes, and perhaps a spot on the cheek-bone and the nose where the
smut has been rubbed off. Some of the little children
were also blackened, and none were over-clad, their
light and airy costume consisting of a calico shirt
reaching only to the waist. Boys eight or ten years old
sometimes had an additional garment,——a pair of
castaway miner's overalls wide enough and ragged
enough for extravagant ventilation. The larger girls
and younger women were arrayed in showy calico,
and wore jaunty straw hats, gorgeously ribboned,
and glowed among the blackened and blanketed old
crones like scarlet tanagers in a flock of blackbirds.
The women, seated on the steps and platform of the
traders' shops, could hardly be called loafers, for
they had berries to sell, basketfuls of huckleberries,
large yellow salmon-berries, and bog raspberries
that looked wondrous fresh and clean amid the sur-

rounding squalor. After patiently waiting for purchasers until hungry, they ate what they could not sell, and went away to gather more.

Yonder you see a canoe gliding out from the shore, containing perhaps a man, a woman, and a child or two, all paddling together in natural, easy rhythm. They are going to catch a fish, no difficult matter, and when this is done their day's work is done. Another party puts out to capture bits of driftwood, for it is easier to procure fuel in this way than to drag it down from the outskirts of the woods through rocks and bushes. As the day advances, a fleet of canoes may be seen along the shore, all fashioned alike, high and long beak-like prows and sterns, with lines as fine as those of the breast of a duck. What the mustang is to the Mexican *vaquero*, the canoe is to these coast Indians. They skim along the shores to fish and hunt and trade, or merely to visit their neighbors, for they are sociable, and have family pride remarkably well developed, meeting often to inquire after each other's health, attend potlatches and dances, and gossip concerning coming marriages, births, deaths, etc. Others seem to sail for the pure pleasure of the thing, their canoes decorated with handfuls of the tall purple epilobium.

Yonder goes a whole family, grandparents and all,

making a direct course for some favorite stream and camp-ground. They are going to gather berries, as the baskets tell. Never before in all my travels, north or south, had I found so lavish an abundance of berries as here. The woods and meadows are full of them, both on the lowlands and mountains—huckleberries of many species, salmon-berries, blackberries, raspberries, with service-berries on dry open places, and cranberries in the bogs, sufficient for every bird, beast, and human being in the territory and thousands of tons to spare. The huckleberries are especially abundant. A species that grows well up on the mountains is the best and largest, a half-inch and more in diameter and delicious in flavor. These grow on bushes three or four inches to a foot high. The berries of the commonest species are smaller and grow almost everywhere on the low grounds on bushes from three to six or seven feet high. This is the species on which the Indians depend most for food, gathering them in large quantities, beating them into a paste, pressing the paste into cakes about an inch thick, and drying them over a slow fire to enrich their winter stores. Salmon-berries and service-berries are preserved in the same way.

A little excursion to one of the best huckleberry-fields adjacent to Wrangell, under the direction of the Collector of Customs, to which I was invited, I greatly enjoyed. There were nine Indians in the party, mostly women and children going to gather huckle-berries. As soon as we had arrived at the chosen camp-ground on the bank of a trout stream, all ran into the bushes and began eating berries before any-thing in the way of camp-making was done, laughing and chattering in natural animal enjoyment. The Collector went up the stream to examine a meadow at its head with reference to the quantity of hay it might yield for his cow, fishing by the way. All the In-dians except the two eldest boys who joined the Col-lector, remained among the berries.

The fishermen had rather poor luck, owing, they said, to the sunny brightness of the day, a complaint seldom heard in this climate. They got good exercise, however, jumping from boulder to boulder in the brawling stream, running along slippery logs and through the bushes that fringe the bank, casting here and there into swirling pools at the foot of cascades, imitating the tempting little skips and whirls of flies so well known to fishing parsons, but perhaps still better known to Indian boys. At the lake-basin the Collector, after he had surveyed his hay-meadow, went around it to the inlet of the lake with his brown pair of attendants to try their luck, while I botanized

in the delightful flora which called to mind the cool
sphagnum and carex bogs of Wisconsin and Canada.
Here I found many of my old favorites the heath-
worts—kalmia, pyrola, chiogenes, huckleberry,
cranberry, etc. On the margin of the meadow darling
linnæa was in its glory; purple panicled grasses in full
flower reached over my head, and some of the carices
and ferns were almost as tall. Here, too, cn the edge
of the woods I found the wild apple tree, the first I
had seen in Alaska. The Indians gather the fruit, small
and sour as it is, to flavor their fat salmon. I never saw
a richer bog and meadow growth anywhere. The
principal forest-trees are hemlock, spruce, and
Nootka cypress, with a few pines (*P. contorta*) on the
margin of the meadow, some of them nearly a hundred feet high, draped with gray usnea, the bark also
gray with scale lichens.

We met all the berry-pickers at the lake, except-
ing only a small girl and the camp-keeper. In their
bright colors they made a lively picture among the
quivering bushes, keeping up a low pleasant chanting
as if the day and the place and the berries were according to their own hearts. The children carried
small baskets, holding two or three quarts; the women two large ones swung over their shoulders. In
the afternoon, when the baskets were full, all started

back to the camp-ground, where the canoe was left. We parted at the lake, I choosing to follow quietly the stream through the woods. I was the first to arrive at camp. The rest of the party came in shortly afterwards, singing and humming like heavy-laden bees. It was interesting to note how kindly they held out handfuls of the best berries to the little girl, who welcomed them all in succession with smiles and merry words that I did not understand. But there was no mistaking the kindliness and serene good nature.

While I was at Wrangell the chiefs and head men of the Stickeen tribe got up a grand dinner and entertainment in honor of their distinguished visitors, three doctors of divinity and their wives, fellow passengers on the steamer with me, whose object was to organize the Presbyterian church. To both the dinner and dances I was invited, was adopted by the Stickeen tribe, and given an Indian name (Ancoutahan) said to mean adopted chief. I was inclined to regard this honor as being unlikely to have any practical value, but I was assured by Mr. Vanderbilt, Mr. Young, and others that it would be a great safeguard while I was on my travels among the different tribes of the archipelago. For travelers without an Indian name might be killed and robbed without the offender being called to account as long as the crime was kept secret from the whites; but, being adopted by the Stickeens, no one belonging to the other tribes would dare attack me, knowing that the Stickeens would hold them responsible.

The dinner-tables were tastefully decorated with flowers, and the food and general arrangements were in good taste, but there was no trace of Indian dishes. It was mostly imported canned stuff served Boston fashion. After the dinner we assembled in Chief Shakes's large block-house and were entertained with lively examples of their dances and amusements, carried on with great spirit, making a very novel barbarous durbar. The dances seemed to me wonderfully like those of the American Indians in general, a monotonous stamping accompanied by hand-clapping, head-jerking, and explosive grunts kept in time to grim drum-beats. The chief dancer and leader scattered great quantities of downy feathers like a snowstorm as blessings on everybody, while all chanted, "Hee-ee-ah-ah, hee-ee-ah-ah," jumping up and down until all were bathed in perspiration.

After the dancing excellent imitations were given of the gait, gestures, and behavior of several animals under different circumstances—walking, hunting, capturing, and devouring their prey, etc. While all were quietly seated, waiting to see what next was go-

ing to happen, the door of the big house was suddenly
thrown open and in bounced a bear, so true to life in
form and gestures we were all startled, though it was
only a bear-skin nicely fitted on a man who was inti-
mately acquainted with the animals and knew how to
imitate them. The bear shuffled down into the middle of the floor and made the motion of jumping into
a stream and catching a wooden salmon that was
ready for him, carrying it out on to the bank, throw-
ing his head around to listen and see if any one was
coming, then tearing it to pieces, jerking his head
from side to side, looking and listening in fear of
hunters' rifles. Besides the bear dance, there were
porpoise and deer dances with one of the party imitating the animals by stuffed specimens with an Indian inside, and the movements were so accurately
imitated that they seemed the real thing.

These animals plays were followed by serious
speeches, interpreted by an Indian woman: "Dear
Brothers and Sisters, this is the way we used to dance.
We liked it long ago when we were blind, we always
danced this way, but now we are not blind. The Good
Lord has taken pity upon us and sent his son, Jesus
Christ, to tell us what to do. We have danced to-day
only to show you how blind we were to like to dance
in this foolish way. We will not dance any more."

Another speech was interpreted as follows: "'Dear Brothers and Sisters,' the chief says, 'this is the way we used to dance and play. We do not wish to do so any more. We will give away all the dance dresses you have seen us wearing, though we value them very highly.' He says he feels much honored to have so many white brothers and sisters at our dinner and plays."

Several short explanatory remarks were made all through the exercises by Chief Shakes, presiding with grave dignity. The last of his speeches concluded thus: "Dear Brothers and Sisters, we have been long, long in the dark. You have led us into strong guiding light and taught us the right way to live and the right way to die. I thank you for myself and all my people, and I give you my heart."

At the close of the amusements there was a potlatch when robes made of the skins of deer, wild sheep, marmots, and sables were distributed, and many of the fantastic head-dresses that had been worn by Shamans. One of these fell to my share.

The floor of the house was strewn with fresh hemlock boughs, bunches of showy wild flowers adorned the walls, and the hearth was filled with huckleberry branches and epilobium. Altogether it was a wonderful show.

I have found southeastern Alaska a good, healthy country to live in. The climate of the islands and shores of the mainland is remarkably bland and temperate and free from extremes of either heat or cold throughout the year. It is rainy, however,—so much so that hay-making will hardly ever be extensively engaged in here, whatever the future may show in the way of the development of mines, forests, and fisheries. This rainy weather, however, is of good quality, the best of the kind I ever experienced, mild in temperature, mostly gentle in its fall, filling the fountains of the rivers and keeping the whole land fresh and fruitful, while anything more delightful than the shining weather in the midst of the rain, the great round sun-days of July and August, may hardly be found anywhere, north or south. An Alaska summer day is a day without night. In the Far North, at Point Barrow, the sun does not set for weeks, and even here in southeastern Alaska it is only a few degrees below the horizon at its lowest point, and the topmost colors of the sunset blend with those of the sunrise, leaving no gap of darkness between. Midnight is only a low noon, the middle point of the gloaming. The thin clouds that are almost always present are then

colored yellow and red, making a striking advertise-
ment of the sun's progress beneath the horizon. The
day opens slowly. The low arc of light steals around to
the northeastward with gradual increase of height
and span and intensity of tone; and when at length
the sun appears, it is without much of that stirring,
impressive pomp, of flashing, awakening, triumphant energy, suggestive of the Bible imagery, a
bridegroom coming out of his chamber and rejoicing
like a strong man to run a race. The red clouds with
yellow edges dissolve in hazy dimness; the islands,
with grayish-white ruffs of mist about them, cast ill-
defined shadows on the glistening waters, and the
whole down-bending firmament becomes pearl-
gray. For three or four hours after sunrise there is
nothing especially impressive in the landscape. The
sun, though seemingly unclouded, may almost be
looked in the face, and the islands and mountains,
with their wealth of woods and snow and varied
beauty of architecture, seem comparatively sleepy
and uncommunicative.

As the day advances toward high noon, the sun-
flood streaming through the damp atmosphere lights
the water levels and the sky to glowing silver.
Brightly play the ripples about the bushy edges of the
islands and on the plume-shaped streaks between

them, ruffled by gentle passing wind-currents. The warm air throbs and makes itself felt as a life-giving, energizing ocean, embracing all the landscape, quickening the imagination, and bringing to mind the life and motion about us—the tides, the rivers, the flood of light streaming through the satiny sky; the marvelous abundance of fishes feeding in the lower ocean; the misty flocks of insects in the air; wild sheep and goats on a thousand grassy ridges; beaver and mink far back on many a rushing stream; Indians floating and basking along the shores; leaves and crystals drinking the sunbeams; and glaciers on the mountains, making valleys and basins for new rivers and lakes and fertile beds of soil.

Through the afternoon, all the way down to the sunset, the day grows in beauty. The light seems to thicken and become yet more generously fruitful without losing its soft mellow brightness. Everything seems to settle into conscious repose. The winds breathe gently or are wholly at rest. The few clouds visible are downy and luminous and combed out fine on the edges. Gulls here and there, winnowing the air on easy wing, are brought into striking relief; and every stroke of the paddles of Indian hunters in their canoes is told by a quick, glancing flash. Bird choirs in

the grove are scarce heard as they sweeten the brooding stillness; and the sky, land, and water meet and
blend in one inseparable scene of enchantment. Then
comes the sunset with its purple and gold, not a narrow arch on the horizon, but oftentimes filling all the
sky. The level cloud-bars usually present are fired on
the edges, and the spaces of clear sky between them
are greenish-yellow or pale amber, while the orderly
flocks of small overlapping clouds, often seen higher
up, are mostly touched with crimson like the out-
leaning sprays of maple-groves in the beginning of an
Eastern Indian Summer. Soft, mellow purple flushes
the sky to the zenith and fills the air, fairly steeping
and transfiguring the islands and making all the water
look like wine. After the sun goes down, the glowing
gold vanishes, but because it descends on a curve
nearly in the same plane with the horizon, the glowing portion of the display lasts much longer than in
more southern latitudes, while the upper colors with
gradually lessening intensity of tone sweep around to
the north, gradually increase to the eastward, and
unite with those of the morning.

The most extravagantly colored of all the sunsets I
have yet seen in Alaska was one I enjoyed on the voyage from Portland to Wrangell, when we were in the

midst of one of the most thickly islanded parts of the Alexander Archipelago. The day had been showery, but late in the afternoon the clouds melted away from the west, all save a few that settled down in narrow level bars near the horizon. The evening was calm and the sunset colors came on gradually, increasing in extent and richness of tone by slow degrees as if requiring more time than usual to ripen. At a height of about thirty degrees there was a heavy cloud-bank, deeply reddened on its lower edge and the projecting parts of its face. Below this were three horizontal belts of purple edged with gold, while a vividly defined, spreading fan of flame streamed upward across the purple bars and faded in a feather edge of dull red. But beautiful and impressive as was this painting on the sky, the most novel and exciting effect was in the body of the atmosphere itself, which, laden with moisture, became one mass of color—a fine translucent purple haze in which the islands with softened outlines seemed to float, while a dense red ring lay around the base of each of them as a fitting border. The peaks, too, in the distance, and the snow-fields and glaciers and fleecy rolls of mist that lay in the hollows, were flushed with a deep, rosy alpenglow of ineffable loveliness. Everything near and far, even the ship, was comprehended in the glorious picture and the general color effect. The mission divines we had aboard seemed then to be truly divine as they gazed transfigured in the celestial glory. So also seemed our bluff, storm-fighting old captain, and his tarry sailors and all.

About one third of the summer days I spent in the Wrangell region were cloudy with very little or no rain, one third decidedly rainy, and one third clear. According to a record kept here of a hundred and forty-seven days beginning May 17 of that year, there were sixty-five on which rain fell, forty-three cloudy with no rain, and thirty-nine clear. In June rain fell on eighteen days, in July eight days, in August fifteen days, in September twenty days. But on some of these days there was only a few minutes' rain, light showers scarce enough to count, while as a general thing the rain fell so gently and the temperature was so mild, very few of them could be called stormy or dismal; even the bleakest, most bedraggled of them all usually had a flush of late or early color to cheer them, or some white illumination about the noon hours. I never before saw so much rain fall with so little noise. None of the summer winds make roaring storms, and thunder is seldom heard. I heard none at all. This

wet, misty weather seems perfectly healthful. There
is no mildew in the houses, as far as I have seen, or any
tendency toward mouldiness in nooks hidden from
the sun; and neither among the people nor the plants
do we find anything flabby or dropsical.

In September clear days were rare, more than
three fourths of them were either decidedly cloudy
or rainy, and the rains of this month were, with one
wild exception, only moderately heavy, and the
clouds between showers drooped and crawled in a
ragged, unsettled way without betraying hints of vio-
lence such as one often sees in the gestures of mountain storm-clouds.

July was the brightest month of the summer, with
fourteen days of sunshine, six of them in uninter-
rupted succession, with a temperature at 7 A.M. of
about 60°, at 12 M., 70°. The average 7 A.M. temperature for June was 54.3°; the average 7 A.M. temperature for July was 55.3°; at 12 M. the average
temperature was 61.45°; the average 7 A.M. temperature for August was 54.12°; 12 M., 61.48°; the average 7 A.M. temperature for September was 52.14°;
and 12 M., 56.12°.

The highest temperature observed here during the
summer was seventy-six degrees. The most remark-

able characteristic of this summer weather, even the brightest of it, is the velvet softness of the atmosphere. On the mountains of California, throughout the greater part of the year, the presence of an atmosphere is hardly recognized, and the thin, white, bodiless light of the morning comes to the peaks and glaciers as a pure spiritual essence, the most impressive of all the terrestrial manifestations of God. The clearest of Alaskan air is always appreciably substantial, so much so that it would seem as if one might test its quality by rubbing it between the thumb and finger. I never before saw summer days so white and so full of subdued lustre.

The winter storms, up to the end of December when I left Wrangell, were mostly rain at a temperature of thirty-five or forty degrees, with strong winds which sometimes roughly lash the shores and carry scud far into the woods. The long nights are then gloomy enough and the value of snug homes with crackling yellow cedar fires may be finely appreciated. Snow falls frequently, but never to any great depth or to lie long. It is said that only once since the settlement of Fort Wrangell has the ground been covered to a depth of four feet. The mercury seldom falls more than five or six degrees below the freezing-point, unless the wind blows steadily from the mainland. Back from the coast, however, beyond the mountains, the winter months are very cold. On the Stickeen River at Glenora, less than a thousand feet above the level of the sea, a temperature of from thirty to forty degrees below zero is not uncommon.

THE STICKEEN
RIVER

THE MOST INTERESTING of the short excursions we made from Fort Wrangell was the one up the Stickeen River to the head of steam navigation. From Mt. St. Elias the Coast Range extends in a broad, lofty chain beyond the southern boundary of the territory, gashed by stupendous cañons, each of which carries a lively river, though most of them are comparatively short, as their highest sources lie in the icy solitudes of the range within forty or fifty miles of the coast. A few, however, of these foaming, roaring streams—the Alsek, Chilcat, Chilcoot, Taku, Stickeen, and perhaps others—head beyond the range with some of the southwest branches of the Mackenzie and Yukon.

The largest side branches of the main-trunk cañ-

ALL THE WORLD OVER

ons of all these mountain streams are still occupied
by glaciers which descend in showy ranks, their
massy, bulging snouts lying back a little distance in
the shadows of the walls, or pushing forward among
the cotton-woods that line the banks of the rivers, or
even stretching all the way across the main cañons,
compelling the rivers to find a channel beneath them.

The Stickeen was, perhaps, the best known of the
rivers that cross the Coast Range, because it was the
best way to the Mackenzie River Cassiar gold-mines.
It is about three hundred and fifty miles long, and is
navigable for small steamers a hundred and fifty miles
to Glenora, and sometimes to Telegraph Creek, fifteen miles farther. It first pursues a westerly course
through grassy plains darkened here and there with
groves of spruce and pine; then, curving southward
and receiving numerous tributaries from the north,
it enters the Coast Range, and sweeps across it
through a magnificent cañon three thousand to five
thousand feet deep, and more than a hundred miles
long. The majestic cliffs and mountains forming the
cañon-walls display endless variety of form and
sculpture, and are wonderfully adorned and enliv-
ened with glaciers and waterfalls, while throughout
almost its whole extent the floor is a flowery landscape garden, like Yosemite. The most striking fea-

tures are the glaciers, hanging over the cliffs, descending the side cañons and pushing forward to the river, greatly enhancing the wild beauty of all the others.

Gliding along the swift-flowing river, the views change with bewildering rapidity. Wonderful, too, are the changes dependent on the seasons and the weather. In spring, when the snow is melting fast, you enjoy the countless rejoicing waterfalls; the gentle breathing of warm winds; the colors of the young leaves and flowers when the bees are busy and wafts of fragrance are drifting hither and thither from miles of wild roses, clover, and honeysuckle; the swaths of birch and willow on the lower slopes following the melting of the winter avalanche snowbanks; the bossy cumuli swelling in white and purple piles above the highest peaks; gray rain-clouds wreathing the outstanding brows and battlements of the walls; and the breaking-forth of the sun after the rain; the shining of the leaves and streams and crystal architecture of the glaciers; the rising of fresh fragrance; the song of the happy birds; and the serene color-grandeur of the morning and evening sky. In summer you find the groves and gardens in full dress; glaciers melting rapidly under sunshine and rain; waterfalls in all their glory; the river rejoicing in its

strength; young birds trying their wings; bears en-
joying salmon and berries; all the life of the cañon
brimming full like the streams. In autumn comes
rest, as if the year's work were done. The rich hazy
sunshine streaming over the cliffs calls forth the last
of the gentians and goldenrods; the groves and thick-
ets and meadows bloom again as their leaves change
to red and yellow petals; the rocks also, and the glaciers, seem to bloom like the plants in the mellow
golden light. And so goes the song, change succeeding change in sublime harmony through all the
wonderful seasons and weather.

My first trip up the river was made in the spring with
the missionary party soon after our arrival at
Wrangell. We left Wrangell in the afternoon and an-
chored for the night above the river delta, and started
up the river early next morning when the heights
above the "Big Stickeen" Glacier and the smooth
domes and copings and arches of solid snow along the
tops of the cañon walls were glowing in the early
beams. We arrived before noon at the old trading-
post called "Buck's" in front of the Stickeen Glacier,
and remained long enough to allow the few passengers who wished a nearer view to cross the river to

the terminal moraine. The sunbeams streaming
through the ice pinnacles along its terminal wall produced a wonderful glory of color, and the broad,
sparkling crystal prairie and the distant snowy fountains were wonderfully attractive and made me pray
for opportunity to explore them.

Of the many glaciers, a hundred or more, that
adorn the walls of the great Stickeen River Cañon,
this is the largest. It draws its sources from snowy
mountains within fifteen or twenty miles of the
coast, pours through a comparatively narrow cañon
about two miles in width in a magnificent cascade,
and expands in a broad fan five or six miles in width,
separated from the Stickeen River by its broad terminal moraine, fringed with spruces and willows.
Around the beautifully drawn curve of the moraine
the Stickeen River flows, having evidently been
shoved by the glacier out of its direct course. On the
opposite side of the cañon another somewhat smaller
glacier, which now terminates four or five miles from
the river, was once united front to front with the
greater glacier, though at first both were tributaries
of the main Stickeen Glacier which once filled the
whole grand cañon. After the main trunk cañon was
melted out, its side branches, drawing their sources
from a height of three or four to five or six thousand

feet, were cut off, and of course became separate glaciers, occupying cirques and branch cañons along the
tops and sides of the walls. The Indians have a tradi-
tion that the river used to run through a tunnel under
the united fronts of the two large tributary glaciers
mentioned above, which entered the main cañon
from either side; and that on one occasion an Indian,
anxious to get rid of his wife, had her sent adrift in a
canoe down through the ice tunnel, expecting that
she would trouble him no more. But to his surprise
she floated through under the ice in safety. All the evi-
dence connected with the present appearance of
these two glaciers indicates that they were united and
formed a dam across the river after the smaller tributaries had been melted off and had receded to a
greater or lesser height above the valley floor.

The big Stickeen Glacier is hardly out of sight ere
you come upon another that pours a majestic crystal
flood through the evergreens, while almost every
hollow and tributary cañon contains a smaller one,
the size, of course, varying with the extent of the
area drained. Some are like mere snow-banks; others, with the blue ice apparent, depend in massive
bulging curves and swells, and graduate into the
river-like forms that maze through the lower forested

regions and are so striking and beautiful that they are admired even by the passing miners with gold-dust in their eyes.

Thirty-five miles above the Big Stickeen Glacier is the "Dirt Glacier," the second in size. Its outlet is a fine stream, abounding in trout. On the opposite side of the river there is a group of five glaciers, one of them descending to within a hundred feet of the river.

Near Glenora, on the northeastern flank of the main Coast Range, just below a narrow gorge called "The Cañon," terraces first make their appearance, where great quantities of moraine material have been swept through the flood-choked gorge and of course outspread and deposited on the first open levels below. Here, too, occurs a marked change in climate and consequently in forests and general appearance of the face of the country. On account of destructive fires the woods are younger and are composed of smaller trees about a foot to eighteen inches in diameter and seventy-five feet high, mostly two-leaved pines which hold their seeds for several years after they are ripe. The woods here are without a trace of those deep accumulations of mosses, leaves, and decaying trunks which make so damp and unclearable a mass in the coast forests. Whole mountain-sides are covered with gray moss and lichens where the forest has been utterly destroyed. The river-bank cottonwoods are also smaller, and the birch and contorta pines mingle freely with the coast hemlock and spruce. The birch is common on the lower slopes and is very effective, its round, leafy, pale-green head contrasting with the dark, narrow spires of the conifers and giving a striking character to the forest. The "tamarac pine" or black pine, as the variety of *P. contorta* is called here, is yellowish-green, in marked contrast with the dark lichen-draped spruce which grows above the pine at a height of about two thousand feet, in groves and belts where it has escaped fire and snow avalanches. There is another handsome spruce hereabouts, *Picea alba*, very slender and graceful in habit, drooping at the top like a mountain hemlock. I saw fine specimens a hundred and twenty-five feet high on deep bottom land a few miles below Glenora. The tops of some of them were almost covered with dense clusters of yellow and brown cones.

We reached the old Hudson's Bay trading-post at Glenora about one o'clock, and the captain informed me that he would stop here until the next morning, when he would make an early start for Wrangell.

At a distance of about seven or eight miles to the northeastward of the landing, there is an outstanding group of mountains crowning a spur from the main chain of the Coast Range, whose highest point rises about eight thousand feet above the level of the sea; and as Glenora is only a thousand feet above the sea, the height to be overcome in climbing this peak is about seven thousand feet. Though the time was short I determined to climb it, because of the advantageous position it occupied for general views of the peaks and glaciers of the east side of the great range.

Although it was now twenty minutes past three and the days were getting short, I thought that by rapid climbing I could reach the summit before sunset, in time to get a general view and a few pencil sketches, and make my way back to the steamer in the night. Mr. Young, one of the missionaries, asked permission to accompany me, saying that he was a good walker and climber and would not delay me or cause any trouble. I strongly advised him not to go, explaining that it involved a walk, coming and going, of fourteen or sixteen miles, and a climb through brush and boulders of seven thousand feet, a fair day's work for a seasoned mountaineer to be done in less than half a day and part of a night. But he insisted that he was a strong walker, could do a mountaineer's day's work in half a day, and would not hinder me in any way.

"Well, I have warned you," I said, "and will not assume responsibility for any trouble that may arise."

He proved to be a stout walker, and we made rapid progress across a brushy timbered flat and up the mountain slopes, open in some places, and in others thatched with dwarf firs, resting a minute here and there to refresh ourselves with huckleberries, which grew in abundance in open spots. About half an hour before sunset, when we were near a cluster of crumbling pinnacles that formed the summit, I had ceased to feel anxiety about the mountaineering strength and skill of my companion, and pushed rapidly on. In passing around the shoulder of the highest pinnacle, where the rock was rapidly disintegrating and the danger of slipping was great, I shouted in a warning voice, "Be very careful here, this is dangerous."

Mr. Young was perhaps a dozen or two yards behind me, but out of sight. I afterwards reproached myself for not stopping and lending him a steadying hand, and showing him the slight footsteps I had made by kicking out little blocks of the crumbling surface, instead of simply warning him to be careful. Only a few seconds after giving this warning, I was startled by a scream for help, and hurrying back, found the missionary face downward, his arms outstretched, clutching little crumbling knobs on the brink of a gully that plunges down a thousand feet or more to a small residual glacier. I managed to get below him, touched one of his feet, and tried to encourage him by saying, "I am below you. You are in no danger. You can't slip past me and I will soon get you out of this."

He then told me that both of his arms were dislocated. It was almost impossible to find available footholds on the treacherous rock, and I was at my wits' end to know how to get him rolled or dragged to a place where I could get about him, find out how much he was hurt, and a way back down the mountain. After narrowly scanning the cliff and making footholds, I managed to roll and lift him a few yards to a place where the slope was less steep, and there I attempted to set his arms. I found, however, that this was impossible in such a place. I therefore tied his arms to his sides with my suspenders and necktie, to prevent as much as possible inflammation from movement. I then left him, telling him to lie still, that I would be back in a few minutes, and that he was now safe from slipping. I hastily examined the ground and saw no way of getting him down except by the

steep glacier gully. After scrambling to an outstanding point that commands a view of it from top to
bottom, to make sure that it was not interrupted by
sheer precipices, I concluded that with great care
and the digging of slight footholds he could be slid
down to the glacier, where I could lay him on his back
and perhaps be able to set his arms. Accordingly, I
cheered him up, telling him I had found a way, but
that it would require lots of time and patience. Digging a footstep in the sand or crumbling rock five or
six feet beneath him, I reached up, took hold of him
by one of his feet, and gently slid him down on his
back, placed his heels in the step, then descended another five or six feet, dug heel notches, and slid him
down to them. Thus the whole distance was made by
a succession of narrow steps at very short intervals,
and the glacier was reached perhaps about midnight.
Here I took off one of my boots, tied a handkerchief
around his wrist for a good hold, placed my heel in his
arm pit, and succeeded in getting one of his arms into
place, but my utmost strength was insufficient to re-
duce the dislocation of the other. I therefore bound it
closely to his side, and asked him if in his exhausted
and trembling condition he was still able to walk.

"Yes," he bravely replied.

So, with a steadying arm around him and many

stops for rest, I marched him slowly down in the star-
light on the comparatively smooth, unfissured surface of the little glacier to the terminal moraine, a
distance of perhaps a mile, crossed the moraine,
bathed his head at one of the outlet streams, and after
many rests reached a dry place and made a brush fire.
I then went ahead looking for an open way through
the bushes to where larger wood could be had, made
a good lasting fire of resiny silver-fir roots, and a leafy
bed beside it. I now told him I would run down the
mountain, hasten back with help from the boat, and
carry him down in comfort. But he would not hear of
my leaving him.

"No, no," he said, "I can walk down. Don't leave
me."

I reminded him of the roughness of the way, his
nerve-shaken condition, and assured him I would not
be gone long. But he insisted on trying, saying on no
account whatever must I leave him. I therefore concluded to try to get him to the ship by short walks
from one fire and resting-place to another. While he
was resting I went ahead, looking for the best way
through the brush and rocks, then returning, got him
on his feet and made him lean on my shoulder while I
steadied him to prevent his falling. This slow, stag-
gering struggle from fire to fire lasted until long after

sunrise. When at last we reached the ship and stood at the foot of the narrow single plank without side rails that reached from the bank to the deck at a considerable angle, I briefly explained to Mr. Young's companions, who stood looking down at us, that he had been hurt in an accident, and requested one of them to assist me in getting him aboard. But strange to say, instead of coming down to help, they made haste to reproach him for having gone on a "wild-goose chase" with Muir.

"These foolish adventures are well enough for Mr. Muir," they said, "but you, Mr. Young, have a work to do; you have a family; you have a church, and you have no right to risk your life on treacherous peaks and precipices."

The captain, Nat Lane, son of Senator Joseph Lane, had been swearing in angry impatience for being compelled to make so late a start and thus encounter a dangerous wind in a narrow gorge, and was threatening to put the missionaries ashore to seek their lost companion, while he went on down the river about his business. But when he heard my call for help, he hastened forward, and elbowed the divines away from the end of the gangplank, shouting in angry irreverence, "Oh, blank! This is no time for preaching! Don't you see the man is hurt?"

He ran down to our help, and while I steadied my trembling companion from behind, the captain kindly led him up the plank into the saloon, and made him drink a large glass of brandy. Then, with a man holding down his shoulders, we succeeded in getting the bone into its socket, notwithstanding the inflammation and contraction of the muscles and ligaments. Mr. Young was then put to bed, and he slept all the way back to Wrangell.

In his mission lectures in the East, Mr. Young oftentimes told this story. I made no record of it in my notebook and never intended to write a word about it; but after a miserable, sensational caricature of the story had appeared in a respectable magazine, I thought it but fair to my brave companion that it should be told just as it happened.

A CRUISE IN THE
CASSIAR

SHORTLY AFTER OUR return to Wrangell the missionaries planned a grand mission excursion up
the coast of the mainland to the Chilcat country,
which I gladly joined, together with Mr. Vanderbilt,
his wife, and a friend from Oregon. The river
steamer Cassiar was chartered, and we had her all to
ourselves, ship and officers at our command to sail
and stop where and when we would, and of course
everybody felt important and hopeful. The main object of the missionaries was to ascertain the spiritual
wants of the warlike Chilcat tribe, with a view to the
establishment of a church and school in their principal village; the merchant and his party were bent on
business and scenery; while my mind was on the
mountains, glaciers, and forests.

This was toward the end of July, in the very brightest and best of Alaska summer weather, when the icy mountains towering in the pearly sky were displayed in all their glory, and the islands at their feet seemed to float and drowse on the shining mirror waters.

After we had passed through the Wrangell Narrows, the mountains of the mainland came in full view, gloriously arrayed in snow and ice, some of the largest and most river-like of the glaciers flowing through wide, high-walled valleys like Yosemite, their sources far back and concealed, others in plain sight, from their highest fountains to the level of the sea.

Cares of every kind were quickly forgotten, and though the Cassiar engines soon began to wheeze and sigh with doleful solemnity, suggesting coming trouble, we were too happy to mind them. Every face glowed with natural love of wild beauty. The islands were seen in long perspective, their forests dark green in the foreground, with varying tones of blue growing more and more tender in the distance; bays full of hazy shadows, graduating into open, silvery fields of light, and lofty headlands with fine arching insteps dipping their feet in the shining water. But every eye was turned to the mountains. Forgotten now were the Chilcats and missions while the word of God was being read in these majestic hieroglyphics blazoned along the sky. The earnest, childish wonderment with which this glorious page of Nature's Bible was contemplated was delightful to see. All evinced eager desire to learn.

"Is that a glacier," they asked, "down in that cañon? And is it all solid ice?"

"Yes."

"How deep is it?"

"Perhaps five hundred or a thousand feet."

"You say it flows. How can hard ice flow?"

"It flows like water, though invisibly slow."

"And where does it come from?"

"From snow that is heaped up every winter on the mountains."

"And how, then, is the snow changed into ice?"

"It is welded by the pressure of its own weight."

"Are these white masses we see in the hollows glaciers also?"

"Yes."

"Are those bluish draggled masses hanging down from beneath the snow-fields what you call the snouts of the glaciers?"

"Yes."

"What made the hollows they are in?"

"The glaciers themselves, just as traveling animals make their own tracks."

"How long have they been there?"

"Numberless centuries," etc. I answered as best I could, keeping up a running commentary on the subject in general, while busily engaged in sketching and noting my own observations, preaching glacial gospel in a rambling way, while the Cassiar, slowly wheezing and creeping along the shore, shifted our position so that the icy cañons were opened to view and closed again in regular succession, like the leaves of a book.

About the middle of the afternoon we were directly opposite a noble group of glaciers some ten in number, flowing from a chain of crater-like snow fountains, guarded around their summits and well down their sides by jagged peaks and cols and curving mural ridges. From each of the larger clusters of fountains, a wide, sheer-walled cañon opens down to the sea. Three of the trunk glaciers descend to within a few feet of the sea-level. The largest of the three, probably about fifteen miles long, terminates in a magnificent valley like Yosemite, in an imposing wall of ice about two miles long, and from three to five hundred feet high, forming a barrier across the valley from wall to wall. It was to this glacier that the ships of the Alaska Ice Company resorted for the ice they carried to San Francisco and the Sandwich Islands, and, I believe, also to China and Japan. To load, they had only to sail up the fiord within a short distance of the front and drop anchor in the terminal moraine.

Another glacier, a few miles to the south of this one, receives two large tributaries about equal in size, and then flows down a forested valley to within a hundred feet or so of sea-level. The third of this low-descending group is four or five miles farther south, and, though less imposing than either of the two sketched above, is still a truly noble object, even as imperfectly seen from the channel, and would of it-self be well worth a visit to Alaska to any lowlander so unfortunate as never to have seen a glacier.

The boilers of our little steamer were not made for sea water, but it was hoped that fresh water would be found at available points along our course where streams leap down the cliffs. In this particular we failed, however, and were compelled to use salt water an hour or two before reaching Cape Fanshawe, the supply of fifty tons of fresh water brought from Wrangell having then given out. To make matters worse, the captain and engineer were not in accord concerning the working of the engines. The captain repeatedly called for more steam, which the engi-neer refused to furnish, cautiously keeping the pres-

sure low because the salt water foamed in the boilers
and some of it passed over into the cylinders, causing
heavy thumping at the end of each piston stroke, and
threatening to knock out the cylinder-heads. At
seven o'clock in the evening we had made only about
seventy miles, which caused dissatisfaction, especially among the divines, who thereupon called a
meeting in the cabin to consider what had better be
done. In the discussions that followed much indigna-
tion and economy were brought to light. We had
chartered the boat for sixty dollars per day, and the
round trip was to have been made in four or five days.
But at the present rate of speed it was found that the
cost of the trip for each passenger would be five or
ten dollars above the first estimate. Therefore, the
majority ruled that we must return next day to
Wrangell, the extra dollars outweighing the mountains and missions as if they had suddenly become
dust in the balance.

Soon after the close of this economical meeting,
we came to anchor in a beautiful bay, and as the long
northern day had still hours of good light to offer, I
gladly embraced the opportunity to go ashore to see
the rocks and plants. One of the Indians, employed as
a deck hand on the steamer, landed me at the mouth
of a stream. The tide was low, exposing a luxuriant

growth of algæ, which sent up a fine, fresh sea smell. The shingle was composed of slate, quartz, and granite, named in the order of abundance. The first land plant met was a tall grass, nine feet high, forming a meadow-like margin in front of the forest. Pushing my way well back into the forest, I found it composed almost entirely of spruce and two hemlocks (*Picea sitchensis, Tsuga heterophylla* and *T. mertensiana*) with a few specimens of yellow cypress. The ferns were developed in remarkable beauty and size—aspidiums, one of which is about six feet high, a woodsia, lomaria, and several species of polypodium. The underbrush is chiefly alder, rubus, ledum, three species of vaccinium, and *Echinopanax horrida*, the whole about from six to eight feet high, and in some places closely intertangled and hard to penetrate. On the opener spots beneath the trees the ground is covered to a depth of two or three feet with mosses of indescribable freshness and beauty, a few dwarf cornels often planted on their rich furred bosses, together with pyrola, coptis, and Solomon's-seal. The tallest of the trees are about a hundred and fifty feet high, with a diameter of about four or five feet, their branches mingling together and making a perfect shade. As the twilight began to fall, I sat down on the mossy instep of a spruce. Not a bush or tree was moving; every leaf seemed hushed in brooding repose. One bird, a thrush, embroidered the silence with cheery notes, making the solitude familiar and sweet, while the solemn monotone of the stream sifting through the woods seemed like the very voice of God, humanized, terrestrialized, and entering one's heart as to a home prepared for it. Go where we will, all the world over, we seem to have been there before.

The stream was bridged at short intervals with picturesque, moss-embossed logs, and the trees on its banks, leaning over from side to side, made high embowering arches. The log bridge I crossed was, I think, the most beautiful of the kind I ever saw. The massive log is plushed to a depth of six inches or more with mosses of three or four species, their different tones of yellow shading finely into each other, while their delicate fronded branches and foliage lie in exquisite order, inclining outward and down the sides in rich, furred, clasping sheets overlapping and felted together until the required thickness is attained. The pedicels and spore-cases give a purplish tinge, and the whole bridge is enriched with ferns and a row of small seedling trees and currant bushes with colored leaves, every one of which seems to have been culled from the woods for this special use, so perfectly do they harmonize in size, shape, and color with the

mossy cover, the width of the span, and the luxuriant, brushy abutments.

Sauntering back to the beach, I found four or five
Indian deck hands getting water, with whom I returned aboard the steamer, thanking the Lord for so
noble an addition to my life as was this one big mountain, forest, and glacial day.

Next morning most of the company seemed un-
comfortably conscience-stricken, and ready to do
anything in the way of compensation for our broken
excursion that would not cost too much. It was not
found difficult, therefore, to convince the captain
and disappointed passengers that instead of creeping
back to Wrangell direct we should make an expiatory
branch-excursion to the largest of the three low-
descending glaciers we had passed. The Indian pilot,
well acquainted with this part of the coast, declared
himself willing to guide us. The water in these fiord
channels is generally deep and safe, and though at
wide intervals rocks rise abruptly here and there,
lacking only a few feet in height to enable them to
take rank as islands, the flat-bottomed Cassiar drew
but little more water than a duck, so that even the
most timid raised no objection on this score. The
cylinder-heads of our engines were the main source
of anxiety; provided they could be kept on all might

yet be well. But in this matter there was evidently
some distrust, the engineer having imprudently informed some of the passengers that in consequence
of using salt water in his frothing boilers the
cylinder-heads might fly off at any moment. To the
glacier, however, it was at length decided we should
venture.

Arriving opposite the mouth of its fiord, we
steered straight inland between beautiful wooded
shores, and the grand glacier came in sight in its granite valley, glowing in the early sunshine and extending a noble invitation to come and see. After we
passed between the two mountain rocks that guard
the gate of the fiord, the view that was unfolded fixed
every eye in wondering admiration. No words can
convey anything like an adequate conception of its
sublime grandeur—the noble simplicity and fineness
of the sculpture of the walls; their magnificent pro-
portions; their cascades, gardens, and forest adorn-
ments; the placid fiord between them; the great
white and blue ice wall, and the snow-laden mountains beyond. Still more impotent are words in telling the peculiar awe one experiences in entering
these mansions of the icy North, notwithstanding it
is only the natural effect of appreciable manifestations of the presence of God.

Standing in the gateway of this glorious temple, and regarding it only as a picture, its outlines may be easily traced, the water foreground of a pale-green color, a smooth mirror sheet sweeping back five or six miles like one of the lower reaches of a great river, bounded at the head by a beveled barrier wall of bluish-white ice four or five hundred feet high. A few snowy mountain-tops appear beyond it, and on either hand rise a series of majestic, pale-gray granite rocks from three to four thousand feet high, some of them thinly forested and striped with bushes and flowery grass on narrow shelves, especially about half way up, others severely sheer and bare and built together into walls like those of Yosemite, extending far beyond the ice barrier, one immense brow appearing beyond another with their bases buried in the glacier. This is a Yosemite Valley in process of formation, the modeling and sculpture of the walls nearly completed and well planted, but no groves as yet or gardens or meadows on the raw and unfinished bottom. It is as if the explorer, in entering the Merced Yosemite, should find the walls nearly in their present condition, trees and flowers in the warm nooks and along the sunny portions of the moraine-covered brows, but the bottom of the valley still covered with water and beds of gravel and mud, and the grand gla-

cier that formed it slowly receding but still filling the
upper half of the valley.

Sailing directly up to the edge of the low, outspread, water-washed terminal moraine, scarce no-
ticeable in a general view, we seemed to be separated
from the glacier only by a bed of gravel a hundred
yards or so in width; but on so grand a scale are all the
main features of the valley, we afterwards found the
distance to be a mile or more.

The captain ordered the Indian deck hands to get
out the canoe, take as many of us ashore as wished to
go, and accompany us to the glacier in case we should
need their help. Only three of the company in the
first place, availed themselves of this rare opportunity of meeting a glacier in the flesh,—Mr. Young,
one of the doctors, and myself. Paddling to the near-
est and driest-looking part of the moraine flat, we
stepped ashore, but gladly wallowed back into the canoe; for the gray mineral mud, a paste made of fine-
ground mountain meal kept unstable by the tides, at
once began to take us in, swallowing us feet foremost
with becoming glacial deliberation. Our next at-
tempt, made nearer the middle of the valley, was suc-
cessful, and we soon found ourselves on firm gravelly
ground, and made haste to the huge ice wall, which
seemed to recede as we advanced. The only difficulty

we met was a network of icy streams, at the largest of which we halted, not willing to get wet in fording. The Indian attendant promptly carried us over on his back. When my turn came I told him I would ford, but he bowed his shoulders in so ludicrously persuasive a manner I thought I would try the queer mount, the only one of the kind I had enjoyed since boyhood days in playing leapfrog. Away staggered my perpendicular mule over the boulders into the brawling torrent, and in spite of top-heavy predictions to the contrary, crossed without a fall. After being ferried in this way over several more of these glacial streams, we at length reached the foot of the glacier wall. The doctor simply played tag on it, touched it gently as if it were a dangerous wild beast, and hurried back to the boat, taking the portage Indian with him for safety, little knowing what he was missing. Mr. Young and I traced the glorious crystal wall, admiring its wonderful architecture, the play of light in the rifts and caverns, and the structure of the ice as displayed in the less fractured sections, finding fresh beauty everywhere and facts for study. We then tried to climb it, and by dint of patient zigzagging and doubling among the crevasses, and cutting steps here and there, we made our way up over the brow and back a mile or two to a height of about seven hundred feet.

The whole front of the glacier is gashed and sculptured into a maze of shallow caves and crevasses, and a bewildering variety of novel architectural forms, clusters of glittering lance-tipped spires, gables, and obelisks, bold outstanding bastions and plain mural cliffs, adorned along the top with fretted cornice and battlement, while every gorge and crevasse, groove and hollow, was filled with light, shimmering and throbbing in pale-blue tones of ineffable tenderness and beauty. The day was warm, and back on the broad melting bosom of the glacier beyond the crevassed front, many streams were rejoicing, gurgling, ringing, singing, in frictionless channels worn down through the white disintegrated ice of the surface into the quick and living blue, in which they flowed with a grace of motion and flashing of light to be found only on the crystal hillocks and ravines of a glacier.

Along the sides of the glacier we saw the mighty flood grinding against the granite walls with tremendous pressure, rounding outswelling bosses, and deepening the retreating hollows into the forms they are destined to have when, in the fullness of appointed time, the huge ice tool shall be withdrawn by the sun. Every feature glowed with intention, reflecting the plans of God. Back a few miles from the front, the glacier is now probably but little more than a thousand feet deep; but when we examine the records on the walls, the rounded, grooved, striated, and polished features so surely glacial, we learn that in the earlier days of the ice age they were all overswept, and that this glacier has flowed at a height of from three to four thousand feet above its present level, when it was at least a mile deep.

Standing here, with facts so fresh and telling and held up so vividly before us, every seeing observer, not to say geologist, must readily apprehend the earth-sculpturing, landscape-making action of flowing ice. And here, too, one learns that the world, though made, is yet being made; that this is still the morning of creation; that mountains long conceived are now being born, channels traced for coming rivers, basins hollowed for lakes; that moraine soil is being ground and outspread for coming plants,— coarse boulders and gravel for forests, finer soil for grasses and flowers,—while the finest part of the grist, seen hastening out to sea in the draining streams, is being stored away in darkness and builded particle on particle, cementing and crystallizing, to make the mountains and valleys and plains of other predestined landscapes, to be followed by still others in endless rhythm and beauty.

Gladly would we have camped out on this grand
old landscape mill to study its ways and works; but
we had no bread and the captain was keeping the
Cassiar whistle screaming for our return. Therefore,
in mean haste, we threaded our way back through the
crevasses and down the blue cliffs, snatched a few
flowers from a warm spot on the edge of the ice,
plashed across the moraine streams, and were pad-
dled aboard, rejoicing in the possession of so blessed
a day, and feeling that in very foundational truth
we had been in one of God's own temples and had
seen Him and heard Him working and preaching like
a man.

Steaming solemnly out of the fiord and down the
coast, the islands and mountains were again passed in
review; the clouds that so often hide the mountain-
tops even in good weather were now floating high
above them, and the transparent shadows they cast
were scarce perceptible on the white glacier fountains. So abundant and novel are the objects of interest in a pure wilderness that unless you are pursuing
special studies it matters little where you go, or how
often to the same place. Wherever you chance to be
always seems at the moment of all places the best;
and you feel that there can be no happiness in this
world or in any other for those who may not be happy

here. The bright hours were spent in making notes and sketches and getting more of the wonderful region into memory. In particular a second view of the mountains made me raise my first estimate of their height. Some of them must be seven or eight thousand feet at the least. Also the glaciers seemed larger and more numerous. I counted nearly a hundred, large and small, between a point ten or fifteen miles to the north of Cape Fanshawe and the mouth of the Stickeen River. We made no more landings, however, until we had passed through the Wrangell Narrows and dropped anchor for the night in a small sequestered bay. This was about sunset, and I eagerly seized the opportunity to go ashore in the canoe and see what I could learn. It is here only a step from the marine algæ to terrestrial vegetation of almost tropical luxuriance. Parting the alders and huckleberry bushes and the crooked stems of the prickly panax, I made my way into the woods, and lingered in the twilight doing nothing in particular, only measuring a few of the trees, listening to learn what birds and animals might be about, and gazing along the dusky aisles.

In the mean time another excursion was being invented, one of small size and price. We might have reached Fort Wrangell this evening instead of anchoring here; but the owners of the Cassiar would then receive only ten dollars fare from each person, while they had incurred considerable expense in fitting up the boat for this special trip, and had treated us well. No, under the circumstances, it would never do to return to Wrangell so meanly soon.

It was decided, therefore, that the Cassiar Company should have the benefit of another day's hire, in visiting the old deserted Stickeen village fourteen miles to the south of Wrangell.

"We shall have a good time," one of the most influential of the party said to me in a semi-apologetic tone, as if dimly recognizing my disappointment in not going on to Chilcat. "We shall probably find stone axes and other curiosities. Chief Kadachan is going to guide us, and the other Indians aboard will dig for us, and there are interesting old buildings and totem poles to be seen."

It seemed strange, however, that so important a mission to the most influential of the Alaskan tribes should end in a deserted village. But divinity abounded nevertheless; the day was divine and there was plenty of natural religion in the newborn landscapes that were being baptized in sunshine, and sermons in the glacial boulders on the beach where we landed.

The site of the old village is on an outswelling strip of ground about two hundred yards long and fifty wide, sloping gently to the water with a strip of gravel and tall grass in front, dark woods back of it, and charming views over the water among the islands—a delightful place. The tide was low when we arrived, and I noticed that the exposed boulders on the beach—granite erratics that had been dropped by the melting ice toward the close of the glacial period—were piled in parallel rows at right angles to the shore-line, out of the way of the canoes that had belonged to the village.

Most of the party sauntered along the shore; for the ruins were overgrown with tall nettles, elder bushes, and prickly rubus vines through which it was difficult to force a way. In company with the most eager of the relic-seekers and two Indians, I pushed back among the dilapidated dwellings. They were deserted some sixty or seventy years before, and some of them were at least a hundred years old. So said our guide, Kadachan, and his word was corroborated by the venerable aspect of the ruins. Though the damp climate is destructive, many of the house timbers were still in a good state of preservation, particularly those hewn from the yellow cypress, or cedar as it is called here. The magnitude of the ruins and the excellence of the workmanship manifest in them was astonishing as belonging to Indians. For example, the first dwelling we visited was about forty feet square, with walls built of planks two feet wide and six inches thick. The ridgepole of yellow cypress was two feet in diameter, forty feet long, and as round and true as if it had been turned in a lathe; and, though lying in the damp weeds, it was still perfectly sound. The nibble marks of the stone adze were still visible, though crusted over with scale lichens in most places. The pillars that had supported the ridgepole were still standing in some of the ruins. They were all, as far as I observed, carved into life-size figures of men, women, and children, fishes, birds, and various other animals, such as the beaver, wolf, or bear. Each of the wall planks had evidently been hewn out of a whole log, and must have required sturdy deliberation as well as skill. Their geometrical truthfulness was admirable. With the same tools not one in a thousand of our skilled mechanics could do as good work. Compared with it the bravest work of civilized backwoodsmen is feeble and bungling. The completeness of form, finish, and proportion of these timbers suggested skill of a wild and positive kind, like that which guides the woodpecker in drilling round holes, and the bee in making its cells.

The carved totem-pole monuments are the most striking of the objects displayed here. The simplest of them consisted of a smooth, round post fifteen or twenty feet high and about eighteen inches in diameter, with the figure of some animal on top—a bear, porpoise, eagle, or raven, about life-size or larger. These were the totems of the families that occupied the houses in front of which they stood. Others supported the figure of a man or woman, life-size or larger, usually in a sitting posture, said to resemble the dead whose ashes were contained in a closed cavity in the pole. The largest were thirty or forty feet high, carved from top to bottom into human and animal totem figures, one above another, with their limbs grotesquely doubled and folded. Some of the most imposing were said to commemorate some event of an historical character. But a telling display of family pride seemed to have been the prevailing motive. All the figures were more or less rude, and some were broadly grotesque, but there was never any feebleness or obscurity in the expression. On the contrary, every feature showed grave force and decision; while the childish audacity displayed in the designs, combined with manly strength in their execution, was truly wonderful.

The colored lichens and mosses gave them a venerable air, while the larger vegetation often found on such as were most decayed produced a picturesque effect. Here, for example, is a bear five or six feet long, reposing on top of his lichen-clad pillar, with paws comfortably folded, a tuft of grass growing in each ear and rubus bushes along his back. And yonder is an old chief poised on a taller pillar, apparently gazing out over the landscape in contemplative mood, a tuft of bushes leaning back with a jaunty air from the top of his weatherbeaten hat, and downy mosses about his massive lips. But no rudeness or grotesqueness that may appear, however combined with the decorations that nature has added, may possibly provoke mirth. The whole work is serious in aspect and brave and true in execution.

Similar monuments are made by other Thlinkit tribes. The erection of a totem pole is made a grand affair, and is often talked of for a year or two beforehand. A feast, to which many are invited, is held, and the joyous occasion is spent in eating, dancing, and the distribution of gifts. Some of the larger specimens cost a thousand dollars or more. From one to two hundred blankets, worth three dollars apiece, are paid to the genius who carves them, while the presents and feast usually cost twice as much, so that only the wealthy families can afford them. I talked

with an old Indian who pointed out one of the carvings he had made in the Wrangell village, for which
he told me he had received forty blankets, a gun, a canoe, and other articles, all together worth about
$170. Mr. Swan, who has contributed much information concerning the British Columbian and Alaskan
tribes, describes a totem pole that cost $2500. They
are always planted firmly in the ground and stand
fast, showing the sturdy erectness of their builders.

While I was busy with my pencil, I heard chopping
going on at the north end of the village, followed by
a heavy thud, as if a tree had fallen. It appeared that
after digging about the old hearth in the first dwelling
visited without finding anything of consequence, the
archæological doctor called the steamer deck hands
to one of the most interesting of the totems and directed them to cut it down, saw off the principal figure,—a woman measuring three feet three inches
across the shoulders,—and convey it aboard the
steamer, with a view to taking it on East to enrich
some museum or other. This sacrilege came near
causing trouble and would have cost us dear had the
totem not chanced to belong to the Kadachan family,
the representative of which is a member of the newly
organized Wrangell Presbyterian Church. Kadachan
looked very seriously into the face of the reverend

doctor and pushed home the pertinent question: "How would you like to have an Indian go to a graveyard and break down and carry away a monument belonging to your family?"

However, the religious relations of the parties and a few trifling presents embedded in apologies served to hush and mend the matter.

Some time in the afternoon the steam whistle called us together to finish our memorable trip. There was no trace of decay in the sky; a glorious sunset gilded the water and cleared away the shadows of our meditations among the ruins. We landed at the Wrangell wharf at dusk, pushed our way through a group of inquisitive Indians, across the two crooked streets, and up to our homes in the fort. We had been away only three days, but they were so full of novel scenes and impressions the time seemed indefinitely long, and our broken Chilcat excursion, far from being a failure as it seemed to some, was one of the most memorable of my life.

THE CASSIAR TRAIL

I MADE A second trip up the Stickeen in August and from the head of navigation pushed inland for general views over dry grassy hills and plains on the Cassiar trail.

Soon after leaving Telegraph Creek I met a merry trader who encouragingly assured me that I was going into the most wonderful region in the world, that "the scenery up the river was full of the very wildest freaks of nature, surpassing all other sceneries either natural or artificial, on paper or in nature."

At the confluence of the first North Fork of the Stickeen I found a band of Toltan or Stick Indians catching their winter supply of salmon in willow traps, set where the fish are struggling in swift rapids on their way to the spawning-grounds. A large supply had already been secured, and of course the Indians were well fed and merry. They were camping in large booths made of poles set on end in the ground, with many binding cross-pieces on which tons of salmon were being dried. The heads were strung on separate poles and the roes packed in willow baskets, all being well smoked from fires in the middle of the floor. The largest of the booths near the bank of the river was about forty feet square. Beds made of spruce and pine boughs were spread all around the walls, on which some of the Indians lay asleep, some were braiding ropes, others sitting and lounging, gossiping and courting, while a little baby was swinging in a hammock. All seemed to be light-hearted and jolly, with work enough and wit enough to maintain health and comfort. . .

One of the most striking of the geological features of this region are immense gravel deposits displayed in sections on the walls of the river gorges. About two miles above the North Fork confluence there is a bluff of basalt three hundred and fifty feet high, and above this a bed of gravel four hundred feet thick, while beneath the basalt there is another bed at least fifty feet thick.

From "Ward's," seventeen miles beyond Tele-graph, and about fourteen hundred feet above sea-level, the trail ascends a gravel ridge to a pine-and-fir-covered plateau twenty-one hundred feet above the sea. Thence for three miles the trail leads through a forest of short, closely planted trees to the second North Fork of the Stickeen, where a still greater deposit of stratified gravel is displayed, a section at least six hundred feet thick resting on a red jaspery formation.

Nine hundred feet above the river there is a slightly dimpled plateau diversified with aspen and willow groves and mossy meadows. At "Wilson's," one and a half miles from the river, the ground is carpeted with dwarf manzanita and the blessed *Linnæa borealis*, and forested with small pines, spruces, and aspens, the tallest fifty to sixty feet high.

From Wilson's to "Caribou," fourteen miles, no water was visible, though the nearly level, mossy ground is swampy-looking. . .

The timber hereabouts is mostly willow or poplar on the low ground, with here and there pine, birch, and spruce about fifty feet high. None seen much exceeded a foot in diameter. Thousand-acre patches have been destroyed by fire. Some of the green trees had been burned off at the root, the raised roots, packed in dry moss, being readily attacked from beneath. A range of mountains about five thousand to six thousand feet high trending nearly north and south for sixty miles is forested to the summit. Only

a few cliff-faces and one of the highest points patched
with snow are treeless. No part of this range as far as
I could see is deeply sculptured, though the general
denudation of the country must have been enormous
as the gravelbeds show.

At the top of a smooth, flowery pass about four
thousand feet above the sea, beautiful Dease Lake
comes suddenly in sight, shining like a broad tranquil
river between densely forested hills and mountains. . .

Dease Creek, a fine rushing stream about forty
miles long and forty or fifty feet wide, enters the lake
from the west, drawing its sources from grassy
mountain-ridges. Thibert Creek, about the same
size, and McDames and Defot Creeks, with their
many branches, head together in the same general
range of mountains or on moor-like tablelands on the
divide between the Mackenzie and Yukon and Stickeen. All these Mackenzie streams had proved rich in
gold. . .

While wandering about the banks of these gold-
besprinkled streams, looking at the plants and mines
and miners, I was so fortunate as to meet an interesting French Canadian, an old *coureur de bois*, who
after a few minutes' conversation invited me to accompany him to his gold-mine on the head of De-

fot Creek, near the summit of a smooth, grassy mountain-ridge, which he assured me commanded extensive views of the region at the heads of Stickeen, Taku, Yukon, and Mackenzie tributaries. Though heavy-laden with flour and bacon, he strode lightly along the rough trails as if his load was only a natural balanced part of his body. Our way at first lay along Thibert Creek, now on gravel benches, now on bed rock, now close down on the bouldery edge of the stream. Above the mines the stream is clear and flows with a rapid current. Its banks are embossed with moss and grass and sedge well mixed with flowers—daisies, larkspurs, solidagos, parnassia, potentilla, strawberry, etc. Small strips of meadow occur here and there, and belts of slender arrowy fir and spruce with moss-clad roots grow close to the water's edge. . . . After crossing many smaller streams with their strips of trees and meadows, bogs and bright wild gardens, we arrived at the Le Claire cabin about the middle of the afternoon. Before entering it he threw down his burden and made haste to show me his favorite flower, a blue forget-me-not, a specimen of which he found within a few rods of the cabin, and proudly handed it to me with the finest respect, and telling its many charms and lifelong associations, showed in every endearing look and touch and gesture that the tender little plant of the mountain wilderness was truly his best-loved darling.

After luncheon we set out for the highest point on the dividing ridge about a mile above the cabin, and sauntered and gazed until sundown, admiring the vast expanse of open rolling prairie-like highlands dotted with groves and lakes, the fountain-heads of countless cool, glad streams.

Le Claire's simple, childlike love of nature, preserved undimmed through a hard wilderness life, was delightful to see. The grand landscapes with their lakes and streams, plants and animals, all were dear to him. In particular he was fond of the birds that nested near his cabin, watched the young, and in stormy weather helped their parents to feed and shelter them. Some species were so confiding they learned to perch on his shoulders and take crumbs from his hand.

A little before sunset snow began to fly, driven by a cold wind, and by the time we reached the cabin, though we had not far to go, everything looked wintry. At half-past nine we ate supper, while a good fire crackled cheerily in the ingle and a wintry wind blew hard. The little log cabin was only ten feet long, eight wide, and just high enough under the roof peak to allow one to stand upright. The bedstead was not wide enough for two, so Le Claire spread the blankets on the floor, and we gladly lay down after our long, happy walk, our heads under the bedstead, our feet against the opposite wall, and though comfortably tired, it was long ere we fell asleep, for Le Claire, finding me a good listener, told many stories of his adventurous life with Indians, bears and wolves, snow and hunger, and of his many camps in the Canadian woods, hidden like the nests and dens of wild animals; stories that have a singular interest to everybody, for they awaken inherited memories of the lang, lang syne when we were all wild. . .

Next morning was cloudy and windy, snowy and cold, dreary December weather in August, and I gladly ran out to see what I might learn. A gray ragged-edged cloud capped the top of the divide, its snowy fringes drawn out by the wind. The flowers, though most of them were buried or partly so, were to some extent recognizable, the bluebells bent over, shining like eyes through the snow, and the gentians, too, with their corollas twisted shut; cassiope I could recognize under any disguise; and two species of dwarf willow with their seeds already ripe, one with comparatively small leaves, were growing in mere cracks and crevices of rock-ledges where the dry snow could not lie. Snowbirds and ptarmigan were flying briskly in the cold wind, and on the edge of a grove I saw a spruce from which a bear had stripped large sections of bark for food.

About nine o'clock the clouds lifted and I enjoyed another wide view from the summit of the ridge of the vast grassy fountain region with smooth rolling features. A few patches of forest broke the monotony of color, and the many lakes, one of them about five miles long, were glowing like windows. Only the highest ridges were whitened with snow, while rifts in the clouds showed beautiful bits of yellow-green sky. The limit of tree growth is about five thousand feet.

Throughout all this region from Glenora to Cassiar the grasses grow luxuriantly in openings in the woods and on dry hillsides where the trees seem to have been destroyed by fire, and over all the broad prairies above the timber-line. A kind of bunch-grass in particular is often four or five feet high, and close enough to be mowed for hay. I never anywhere saw finer or more bountiful wild pasture. Here the caribou feed and grow fat, braving the intense winter cold, often forty to sixty degrees below zero. Winter and summer seem to be the only seasons here. What may fairly be called summer lasts only two or three months, winter nine or ten, for of pure well-defined spring or autumn there is scarcely a trace. Were it not for the long severe winters, this would be a capital stock country, equaling Texas and the prairies of the old West. From my outlook on the Defot ridge I saw thousands of square miles of this prairie-like region drained by tributaries of the Stickeen, Taku, Yukon, and Mackenzie Rivers. . .

A brown, speckled marmot, one of Le Claire's friends, was getting ready for winter. The entrance to his burrow was a little to one side of the cabin door. A well-worn trail led to it through the grass and another to that of his companion, fifty feet away. He was a most amusing pet, always on hand at meal times for bread-crumbs and bits of bacon-rind, came when called, answering in a shrill whistle, moving like a squirrel with quick, nervous impulses, jerking his short flat tail. His fur clothing was neat and clean, fairly shining in the wintry light. The snowy weather that morning must have called winter to mind; for as soon as he got his breakfast, he ran to a tuft of dry grass, chewed it into fuzzy mouthfuls, and carried it to his nest, coming and going with admirable industry, forecast, and confidence. None watching him as we did could fail to sympathize with him; and I fancy that in practical weather wisdom no government forecaster with all his advantages surpasses this little

Alaska rodent, every hair and nerve a weather in-
strument.

I greatly enjoyed this little inland side trip—the
wide views; the miners along the branches of the
great river, busy as moles and beavers; young men
dreaming and hoping to strike it rich and rush home
to marry their girls faithfully waiting; others hoping to clear off weary farm mortgages, and brighten
the lives of the anxious home folk; but most I sup-
pose, just struggling blindly for gold enough to make
them indefinitely rich to spend their lives in aim-
less affluence, honor, and ease. I enjoyed getting
acquainted with the trees, especially the beautiful
spruce and silver fir; the flower gardens and great
grassy caribou pastures; the cheery, able marmot
mountaineer; and above all the friendship and kind-
ness of Mr. Le Claire, whom I shall never forget. Bid-
ding good-bye, I sauntered back to the head of
navigation on the Stickeen, happy and rich without a
particle of obscuring gold-dust care.